PRAISE FOR HILLARY McBRIDE

"McBride's insights are a gift."

—**Kaitlin Curtice**,
author of *Living Resistance*

"Hillary is such a worthy guide, the kind you can trust in the most
dangerous wildernesses of your body and soul and mind."

—**Sarah Bessey**, author of *Jesus Feminist*, editor of the
New York Times bestseller *A Rhythm of Prayer*

"Hillary McBride has this magic in her personal life and clinical
work that disarms you. She gives you insights, keys, and practices
to fall in love with yourself."

—**Lisa Gungor**, musician, author,
and co-conspirator of Sacred Feminine

"Hillary McBride has changed my life through her combination
of powerful intelligence and extraordinary tenderness."

—**Mari Andrew**, author of *My Inner Sky*

"McBride's words are a gift to the world."

—**Ruthie Lindsey**, speaker and
author of *There I Am*

PRACTICES for EMBODIED LIVING

Previous Books by the Author

The Wisdom of Your Body:
Finding Healing, Wholeness, and Connection through Embodied Living

Mothers, Daughters, and Body Image:
Learning to Love Ourselves as We Are

PRACTICES *for* EMBODIED LIVING

Experiencing the Wisdom of Your Body

Hillary L. McBride, PhD

BrazosPress

a division of Baker Publishing Group
Grand Rapids, Michigan

Published by Brazos Press
a division of Baker Publishing Group
Grand Rapids, Michigan
BrazosPress.com

Printed in the United States of America

Library of Congress Cataloging-in-Publication Data
Names: McBride, Hillary L., author.
Title: Practices for embodied living : experiencing the wisdom of your body / Hillary L. McBride, PhD.
Description: Grand Rapids, Michigan : Brazos Press, a division of Baker Publishing Group, [2024]
Identifiers: LCCN 2023020878 | ISBN 9781587436246 (paperback) | ISBN 9781493445042 (ebook)
Subjects: LCSH: Stress (Psychology)—Religious aspects. | Listening—Religious aspects. | Spiritual life. | Mind and body therapies.
Classification: LCC BF575.S75 M393 2023 | DDC 155.9/042—dc23/eng/20230710
LC record available at https://lccn.loc.gov/2023020878

Cover illustrations and interior illustrations by Kelli Laderer.

Interior design by Jane Klein.

Author is represented by The Christopher Ferebee Agency, ChristopherFerebee.com.

Baker Publishing Group publications use paper produced from sustainable forestry practices and post-consumer waste whenever possible.

24 25 26 27 28 29 30   7 6 5 4 3 2 1

CONTENTS

AN INVITATION to BE HERE NOW

There is more wisdom in the hands holding this book,
than in the pages of the book the hands are holding.

Your body is a messenger

A web of connection

A key to resistance

A well of resources

A soft place to land

An invitation to be here now

I remember the first time I understood as an adult that my body was saying something worth listening to, something that deserved to be heard.

During our session, my therapist asked me to pay attention to how I was sitting in the chair. I didn't understand the question. Then, she showed me how I used to sit in the chair when I first started working with her: her contorted posture was like a mirror for my inner experience; my body was communicating the pain I did not have words for. As my experience of myself began to change, so did the way I moved through spaces, sat, fed myself, slowed down, sped up, danced, emoted, and rested.

As I continued to experiment with different ways of being in my body, my sense of self continued to change. The once clear line between who I believed myself to be (my mind) and the object that housed my self (my body) began to blur. I started to see that everything that happened to my body happened to me; nothing happened to me that didn't also permeate the experience of being in my body. I was becoming my body, and it was making me more of myself.

We are born with no other option than to be a body. But soon, we learn that being a body can be scary, even dangerous. Our bodies are judged, are hurt, get sick, are mysterious to us, or seem to be too much for the people around us because we have wants, reactions, longings, desires, or feelings.

We learn, sometimes on purpose but often without even knowing it is happening, to draw a line between our minds and our bodies, saying that the body is "not me." This can happen so early that we can wake up in our adult lives and believe, deeply, that our minds are the places where our selves exist.

To be so separate from ourselves costs us so much: connection to ourselves and others, the joy of pleasure, the sense of aliveness, the ability to be here now. No matter where else we have to go, or where we try to be, our senses are the doorway back into the present—our constant invitation to be exactly where we are.

BEING A BODY

One of the ways this separation occurs is through how we come to identify where our "self-ness" lives. We come to think of our "self" or "me-ness" as living in our heads or in our

minds. This idea has a few thousand years of Western cultural history and philosophy behind it, and it shapes many of our societal assumptions and ways of speaking. It keeps us relating to our body as a thing or an object that carries around our mind, which is thought of as our true self. The experts call this viewing the *body as object*. Instead, embodiment is a pathway to reclaim our body as a place that holds just as much of our "self" of our "me-ness" as our minds and thoughts do. Instead of our body being a vehicle for the self, a puppet animated by our mind, embodiment invites us to see that we are our bodies. Our self-ness exists just as much in our toes, digestive track, beating heart, coordinated movements on the dance floor, memories of smell and sound, and laughter as it does in our thoughts and mind. Our bodies are always communicating about likes and dislikes, holding ancestral memories, communicating insight about safety, and giving us cues about what is unfinished from our past that needs to be expressed. The experts call this *body as subject*. Our bodies are dynamic, alive, natural, wild, and full of mystery. I am my body. You are your body. **A BODY IS NOT JUST A THING YOU HAVE; IT IS WHO YOU ARE.**

HOW TO USE THIS BOOK

This book is for where you are, exactly as you are. It is designed to help you be even more of who you are and to learn that being in your body can be a safe, rich, alive, and connecting place. As I wrote this book, I imagined it as a series of doors that open you toward yourself, providing you with invitations and ideas about how to experience yourself more fully as a body.

If you have read my book *The Wisdom of Your Body*, I hope that this provides broader and deeper practices to accompany you on your journey through that book. If you have not read *The Wisdom of Your Body* and want to access more of the ideas behind these practices, that book is a great place to start. Or it could be a place to head when you set this one down for a while. The series of practices in this book will be structured to follow the chapters in *The Wisdom of Your Body*, which could also make it a lovely accompaniment.

If you wanted to read *The Wisdom of Your Body*, but found it too long, dense, or wordy, rest assured that this book will provide you with the same essence but will be much more accessible and practical.

You might read this book day by day on your own, as part of or instead of a regular prayer or spiritual practice or writing time (perhaps adding exercises into what you are already doing or picking an exercise to do and following it by writing about what happened for you). Or you might pick a specific practice and do it over and over and over, day by day, to see how it connects you to yourself over time.

One option to try is reading through this book in its entirety and taking note of what jumps out at you so you can return to it in a quiet moment or when you're longing to go deeper into self-exploration. This may happen as your shoulders pull you forward toward the pages or as you notice a surge of energy in your core and face.

Another idea is to practice the exercises from start to finish and see what their effect is on your sense of self, returning to the ones you need in a moment of emotional intensity when you want to shift out of how you feel or when you need help staying with what you are feeling to get through to the other side.

You could leave this book on your coffee table or office waiting room, you could take photos of the pages, or you could fold down the corners to return to what anchors you most. I can imagine you may have ideas all your own as you turn the pages and try to stay in contact with what you feel inside, trusting that the insight you find there will be exactly what you need.

You might also read this book with other people. Our bodies and the stories they hold are different from one another. Still, the body is the great unifier. All of us are bodies and can practice remembering that in a way that draws us more deeply into the present and connects us with each other. You might use exercises in this book to start or end your small group, church services or spiritual gathering, group therapy, staff workshop, consciousness-raising group, book club, ceremony, family meeting, retreats, or community gathering. You also might work systematically through these practices with a group you already meet with, or you could start a group simply for the purpose of saying yes to these invitations together. (See the appendix for ideas on how to facilitate a gathering using the practices in this book or how to use this book in groups that are already reading *The Wisdom of Your Body*.) As you meet, continue to adapt these invitations and build your own practices.

None of the work we do to heal occurs in isolation. The work of healing is held in a web of wisdom, the product of wholeness, integration, and interconnection. The following activities and exercises are ones I have collected, created, and adapted over years of doing my own embodiment work and learning from others. You may recognize some of them from work you've done in your therapist's office or clinical trainings, from your workshop experiences, or from your psychology books. Although what follows is my interpretation of these exercises, a debt of gratitude is owed to the collective community of therapists, researchers, body workers, and clinicians who have inspired them. What I have been offered I have adapted and now offer to you so that you might adapt it and use it to create something of your own. Use what you encounter so that it works for you, giving away the experiences of meaning and healing to your community and to those you love and leaving the rest behind. Not all of these practices will be suitable for every reader, every body, or every season or state you arrive in. As you read and experiment, notice what does not seem fitting, and feel free to adjust it or move on to something else. It would be my joy to meet you somewhere in the world with a copy of this book in your hand and to see the way you had scribbled through it, crossed out words to replace with your own, and added pages in for something you needed that I had missed.

This work is most like a medicine when it meets your needs as an individual and as a community, when it comes off the pages and into your tissues, and when it helps you know, through experience, that your body has something important to say.

EXPLORING EMBODIMENT

Life is complex—it is beautiful and painful and mysterious.
And life happens in and through our bodies.

So bodies, and how we relate to them, are beautiful and painful and mysterious.

> **Bodies are the place** of our pain, hunger, and fear. Bodies are the place where we experience loneliness, social rejection, illness, and death. Bodies are here, even when we don't want to be here.

> **Bodies are also** where we feel alive, joy, pleasure, and the spark of creativity. It is in our bodies that we experience connection, vitality, being held, sensuality, self-expression, and presence. Our bodies are here, especially when here is a place we want to be.

WE OFTEN DISTANCE OURSELVES FROM WHAT IS PAINFUL ABOUT BEING A BODY, ONLY TO FIND THAT WE LOSE WHAT MAKES US FEEL ALIVE.

What we often didn't learn growing up is that we *inherit* our fraught relationships with our bodies. Being a body is complicated because we swim in a cultural story that has been put together over millennia. That story tells us that being a body is dangerous and that our bodies need to be controlled. This story keeps us from what is true.

We start to believe what we are told: our bodies are the problem, the source of our pain, the cause of our trauma, and somehow the best

OBJECTIFIC
TH
BODY HIERARCH
PLATO

ARTES

N

IGHTENMENT

T CULTURE

GNOSTICISM

way to get power. This makes it very hard to believe that we are bodies and to feel at ease in our bodies. We begin to live in our minds, believing that our *selves* exists mostly, or only, in our thinking and that our thinking happens in our brains. Our bodies are just meat puppets carrying our selves around. This is disembodiment.

The idea of embodiment gives us a better way of thinking about our humanness.

Embodiment is the experience of being a body, and that experience is shaped by each person's social context.

EMBODIMENT helps to heal the mind-body divide, the self-other distance, and the person-land schism. Embodiment doesn't have to be learned, for we are born into it; it only has to be remembered.

I was born EMBODIED.

All I have to do is remember what was mine all along.

✳ EMBODIMENT INVITES US TO SEE THAT

Our bodies are more than our appearances.

Our bodies shape our thinking.

Our selves exist in our feet and femurs and forearms, not just in our frontal lobes.

Our bodies connect us to our ancestors, our pasts, and all other living beings.

Our bodies are where life happens; being in our bodies brings us into life.

CHECKING IN

Take a few minutes to encounter how it is to be a body.

Without altering anything, notice your posture. Notice the temperature of your body and the room. You can ask yourself, Are you hungry or full? Do you have to go to the bathroom? How tired are you? Where do you feel pain? What parts of your body can you not feel at all? What are you touching? If you notice an emotion, where do you sense it? Does the left side of your body feel the same as the right side? Does the front feel the same as the back? Do you sense that you could take action right now? If so, where does that sense of creating movement live?

OBJECT VERSUS SUBJECT

We can see our bodies as things (objects), or we can experience our bodies as living beings (subjects).

Try touching the skin on the back of your hand like it is a thing. Poke it, pinch it, rest something on it, scrub it.

Try touching the skin on the back of your hand like it is alive. Gaze at it, rub it, talk to it, ask it a question.

What differences did you notice between those two ways of relating to your hand? How did your thoughts change? What feelings did you have with each way of relating?

You could also try this with your foot, your face, or your belly. See what happens with different areas of your body when you treat them like a subject or an object.

GET CURIOUS

Think of something you feel curious about, or remember a time when you felt openhearted, curious, and nonjudgmental. Allow yourself to notice how that feels in your body. (You might lean forward slightly, tilt your chin up, or feel your shoulders relax.) When you feel openhearted, curious, and nonjudgmental, think of which questions you might like to ask your body. Notice how it feels to want to know.

OUR BODIES TELL THE STORIES

Our bodies tell the stories of what we have been through and who we come from. Our bodies invite us to remember that we have ancestors and that we share a common humanity with other people. If you have a mirror or a photo of yourself, look at your features or your body as a whole, and answer the following questions:

Who do you look like (either specific people or groups of people)?

Who has hair like yours, a face shape like yours, eyes like yours?

Who walks like you do?

What experience did you have recently that you felt alone in?

Even if the specifics of your feelings and experiences are unique to you, in the history of the world, other people have felt those things and experienced those things too. Imagine them next to you.

Notice how it feels to sense your body as the portal to connection.

WRITE THE STORY

Write the story of your body in five sentences.

EMBODIMENT CHECK-IN

Embodiment—which is connected, freeing, and healing—gives us agency, comfort and connection, the experience and expression of desire, and attuned self-care, and it helps us experience our bodies as subjects instead of objects.

Ask yourself the following questions, or try the following prompts.

Agency

What parts of my bodily experience can I have control over?

What makes me feel powerful?

Try making a shift in posture or movement right now, just because you can.

Try taking a form that feels solid, sturdy, powerful, or action-oriented.

Try getting as big as you can as a body, taking up as much space as possible.

Comfort and Connection

What brings me comfort? What connects me to my experience of being a body?

What connects me to others?

How can I offer myself comfort right now?

Practice holding yourself or rubbing your shoulders.

Try touching something that is soft or wrapping yourself up in a sweater or blanket.

Experiencing and Expressing Desire

What do I want? What does my desire feel like from the inside out?

Complete this sentence: "I feel pleasure when ..."

What does it feel like to give myself what I want?

Complete this sentence: "My wildest dream is ..."

Name what you desire, or write a list of desires.

Caring for Ourselves with Attunement

What are the signals that I need care from myself?

What is a bodily cue I have that I could listen to right now?

Pick something from the following list and try to prioritize it over the next twenty-four hours. Notice when you need to: feed yourself, change your posture, hydrate, stop eating, get up and move, rest, soothe yourself, emote, or feel touch.

What fills me up? Who are the people I like to be around?

Complete this sentence: "If I were to care for my bodily self like I would care for a child, I would . . ."

Try getting a full glass of water, and as you drink it, notice what tells you that it's time to stop drinking. Try to sense where that information comes from.

The Subjective Body

What could I value about my body besides how I look? What experiences do I value having as a body?

Complete this sentence: "I can respect my body for . . ."

Complete this sentence: "Because of my body I can experience . . ."

What does my body long to be asked?

Try imagining that your sense of self exists outside of you, hovering around your body as a warm ball of light. Imagine that it enters through the top of your head. How does that feel?

Imagine that it shifts into your chest, then belly, then hips, then feet and hands. How does that feel?

RELATIONAL CIRCLE

When the practices in this book become challenging or bring challenging memories to the surface, who do you want to believe is by your side? These companions can be real or imagined, in your relational circle or known from afar.

 Gather photos of these companions, write down their names, and think of what they could say that you would need to hear in a difficult moment.

BREATH EXERCISE

Try placing your hands on your body and saying to yourself, "This is my body; here I am."

Let your hands linger there for three breaths. Then move your hands across your body, again repeating the phrase, "This is my body; here I am." Try doing this and touching every area of your body, leaving nothing out. If that is too difficult, start with what you can manage and stretch yourself a little bit each time you return to the practice. Try different phrases, and see what works.

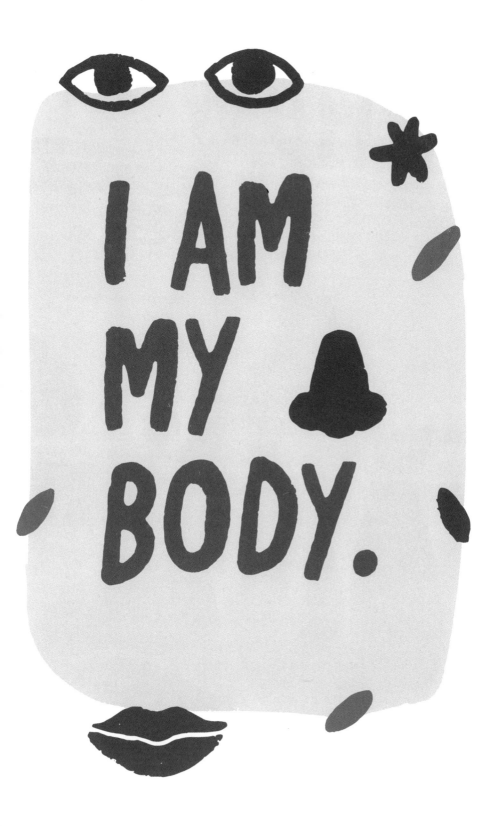

BECOME DISEMBODIED

LIES ABOUT our BODiES, and HOW to FiND OUR WAY HOME

We are born embodied. But the thing we have the most practice learning is disembodiment. Cultural stories make it seem like our bodies are dangerous, a problem to be managed, vile and untrustworthy, and something to be controlled.

HERE ARE SOME UNTRUTHS WE FACE IN WESTERN CULTURE:

You are not your body.

You need to subdue and control your body because it is dangerous.

Some bodies are better than others.

Bodies must present within rigid binaries of gender.

Ideal women have sexual, young, thin, and fertile bodies.

Bodies are impure, and pleasure is sinful.

Appearance is all that matters about your body.

You should change your body.

Fat bodies are unhealthy.

Others get to decide what is best for your body.

Bodies get in the way of pure and right thinking.

What stories do you want to add?

Which body stories have made it most difficult to be in your body?

AS YOU ARE IMAGINING THOSE STORIES, picture them as a layer of fabric that someone wrapped around you.

You might wrap yourself in a series of scarves, blankets, or coats, and as you name the untruths, take the layers of fabric off one by one to represent taking off those stories. Notice how it feels.

Imagine the stories have been like a film covering your skin. Wipe your hand across your whole body, shaking your hands as you get close to the ground, symbolically wiping off the stories. You could also try taking a bath or a shower, imagining that you are washing them off.

Try writing the stories on paper and either burning them in a fire or lighting them with a match in a heatproof bowl or burying them in the ground. You could use a waterproof marker to write the stories or words on a rock and then throw them into a body of water. As you do this, imagine extending some gratitude to the elements for helping you process and deal with the things that you were never meant to carry.

Think of how it feels to see these stories. Put on a song that captures that feeling, and dance the feeling off or out of your body, taking movement or making shapes that help you feel like you can express the feeling without words. You can also pick a motion, form of movement, or posture that helps you feel like you can metabolize the feeling and the message, using up all the energy of the emotion it caused in you.

THREE PATHWAYS

We learn to experience ourselves as a body through three pathways:

MENTAL: the stories we think and perpetuate about bodies

SOCIAL: the social landscape around us

PHYSICAL: the physical experiences we have

Together, these pathways shape whether the experience we have of our body is a safe, caring, and attuned one or whether we feel powerless, disconnected, and constricted.

Mental

What do I want to think about my body?

What do I want to think about bodies in general?

What would I tell my younger self about bodies?

As you write, think, or talk about these questions, notice your emotions.

Pick a color for what this feels like. Make a movement or take a form (place your body in a shape) that represents what it might feel like to have freedom in the way you think about your body.

Social

Which places and groups of people allow me to feel most at ease in my skin?

With whom do I feel most connected and calm or equal and respected?

What do I want to stand against? What do I want to stand for?

Who am I glad to be like? Who do I want to be like?

As you write, think, or talk about these questions, notice your emotions.

Pick a sound for what that feels like. Make a movement or a form (a shape with your body) for what it might be like to feel belonging and social safety.

Physical

What kind of movement do I look forward to doing?

What kind of movements leave me feeling at ease or satisfied afterward?

Complete this sentence: "I am safe to move exactly how I want to move when . . ."

Try different kinds of movement that come naturally to most children. Put on a song and skip, hop on one or both feet, crawl on your hands and knees, jump up and down, twirl in circles, or roll around on the ground.

If you have children in your life or a friend to play with, try naming different animals and then acting out their movements.

EMBODIMENT STORIES

The following stories open doors back into embodiment:

> My body is mine; my body is me.
> My body and my mind can be friends.
> My body is a resource.
> My body is a resistance.
> My body is a sanctuary.

When we can access one of these stories, it's easier to access the others. These stories don't need to be accessed one after the other, but if you need somewhere to start, start at the top. Below are exercises and questions to help you connect with each story.

My Body Is Mine; My Body Is Me

Put your hands on your body and say, "This belongs to me," or say any other words that feel right, like "This is my body" or "Here I am." Try moving your hands across your body, lingering if you are able on parts of your body that need to remember they are yours.

Consider: What would have to happen for you to believe that your body is you?

Move your hands across the surface of your body slowly and say to yourself, "This is me."

Notice what it feels like to be you today. Try turning that into a form or movement.

Complete this sentence: "If my body is mine, then ..."

Complete this sentence: "Because my body is me, I can ..."

My Body and My Mind Can Be Friends

Imagine that your nondominant hand is your thinking self and that your dominant hand is your sensing, bodily self. Try holding them side by side, noticing how the distance feels. When you're ready, experiment with bringing them closer together, clasping your hands and interweaving your fingers.

What do your thoughts long to hear from your sensing body? What does your bodily self long to hear from your thinking self?

Complete the following sentences:
"It makes me feel loved when a friend ..." (try doing that for yourself)

"I long to hear from those I love that I ..." (try saying this to yourself)

When talking about your bodily self, try talking about your body like a person you love being with. For example, try giving your body pronouns, giving your body a nickname, or writing a note to your body to stick on your bathroom mirror.

My Body Is a Resource

Either with your touch or with your mind, bring attention to each of the body parts listed below, noticing what they offer to your human experience and perhaps thanking them for each of the resources they give you.

Here are some affirmations to offer to different parts of your body.

Feet

Thank you for moving me through space.
You help me get away from what doesn't serve me.
You help me move toward what I love.
I couldn't be balanced without you.

Hands

My extension into life, you help me be open and to receive.
You are a pathway for communication, telling others what I think, want, and don't want.
Thank you for sending love into the world through tender touch and care.
You can wrap yourself around me and offer me kindness.

Spine

You hold me up, especially in moments when I need courage.
Thank you for being both flexible and sturdy. You help me stay solid and clear while also being adaptive and fluid.
You remind me that I can lift myself up and take up more space.
Thank you for offering me support without me even asking you to.

Heart

You are working hard to make sure that every part of me has what it needs.

Thank you for being there right from the beginning.

You remind me that I can keep going, even when I feel weary.

I can listen to what you say about how scared or excited I am.

You show me that there is balance between contraction and expansion.

Belly

Thank you for taking in what I need to fill me up.

You remind me that I know, instinctively, how to take in what is good for me and how to send away what isn't good for me.

You are always telling me when I need more or when I've had enough.

When you expand and relax, I know I am safe and comfortable.

Lungs and Breath

Because of you, I can remember that rhythm lives in my body.

You know how to release what isn't good for me to hold on to anymore.

You know how to be open and how to take in what I need.

Building Bodily Resources

Think of a feeling or situation that gets you stuck. Is there a way your body can get you unstuck? Try practicing it now, even if you don't need it.

If you feel trapped, try getting up and walking around.

If you feel scared, try holding your own hand.

If you feel insecure and small, try getting big and tall and wide.

If you feel blocked creatively, try wiggling around.

If you feel disorganized, use clear, precise, rigid movements.

If you feel tense, contract your muscles and then flop them around.

If you feel too rigid, try moving your hips in circles.

My Body Is a Resistance

Reflect on the following questions:

When I am in a place of security and stability, what do I want to resist?

How have I been restricted as a body by the social scripts around me?

How can I interfere with these social scripts as a body, right now or in my day to day?

Complete this sentence: "I want to be able to share power with . . ."

Try taking a form or movement for what equality feels like.

My Body Is a Sanctuary

Remember a time you felt alive, loved, or connected. If you can, hold it in your mind and remember what it felt like in your body. Notice what happens now, in your body, as you remember that.

Complete this sentence: "If I believed my body was completely loved, then . . ."

Complete this sentence: "When I know that my body, all bodies, are sacred, then . . ."

What is an object that represents Love or Life? Imagine placing it inside your rib cage.

It is never too late to learn how to come back home to myself.

THE BODY OVERWHELMED

HEALiNG THE BODY FROM STRESS AND TRAUMA

Stress, as a process, is not categorically bad. It is a good and healthy bodily response to something we perceive is challenging. Without enough of it in our bodies, we don't meet challenges in life with the resources we need. But when it is not used to help us meet challenges, and when too much of it is left lingering in our bodies, the body pays the price, and we can find it hard to be present and at ease. If things don't change, then the stress is too much to bear, and our bodily systems can start to break down.

A stressful event becomes trauma when our capacity to manage the situation, care for ourselves, and stay connected to our resources becomes overwhelmed, leaving us feeling powerless and disconnected. The situation feels unresolved to our nervous systems, and our bodies continue responding as if the event is still happening, even if we know on some level that it ended a long time ago.

When not faced with interference, and when we get the social support and connection we are designed for, our bodies

THE STRESS-RESPONSE STAIRCASE

Our bodies take a reliable path when we are facing stress and trauma. Designed to be able to live our lives with ease when we are safe, when we are presented with a stressor, a threat, or the memory of a threat, our bodies can jump to any of the steps in the following figure to try to keep us safe. This is unconscious and meant for our survival. If we don't get the care we need, or if the traumas are ongoing, then we can get stuck on one step or straddling a few.

The good news is that our nervous systems—the unconscious process living inside of us connecting brain and body and determining where on the staircase we rest—is adaptable, always capable of learning, healing, and getting updated.

Our bodies come out of trauma responses following the same path that they took as the trauma happened. We come up the staircase the same way we went down it. Our bodies can be trusted to know the way out; they never skip a step.

know how to resolve the activation that comes from stress and trauma. We just have to trust that resolving stress and trauma might mean that we have to be in our bodies differently than we learned to.

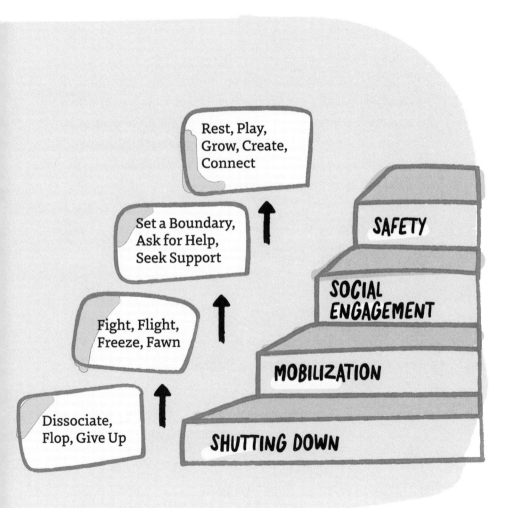

Safety

When I am in safety, how do I know? What in my body tells me I'm feeling safe? What do I notice around me? What are my thoughts like? What can I sense? How does the world seem to me?

Complete this sentence: "When my body is at rest, I can . . ."

Although it can seem like work can be done only when our bodies are actively experiencing a stress response, it can also be challenging to enjoy feelings of rest, ease, play, and connection. When you are in a relaxed state, try to notice everything about what it is like and enjoy it; try to stretch yourself to stay there just a little bit longer than normal.

Social Engagement

When I am slightly activated, how do I know? What in my body tells me that my level of stress is changing? How does my perception of the world change? What do I notice? What do I not notice? What happens to my sense of connection? What does the energy in my throat feel like?

Try humming a tune.
Try swallowing a sip of water and gargling.

If the boundaries we set have not been respected or if our efforts to connect seem to create more feelings of being unsafe, then we can learn ways to indirectly set boundaries or ask for help. We can tell we are trying to set a boundary indirectly if we are irritated or angry that someone continues to do what they do. We can tell that we are trying to ask for help or to connect indirectly when we feel scared, irritated, disappointed, or lonely if we reach out and don't receive care or a response back from a person.

Complete this sentence: "When I am slightly activated, the people I can reach for are…"

Complete this sentence: "The way I reach is…"

Complete this sentence: "When I am slightly activated, my boundaries look and sound like…"

Mobilization

When I am feeling activated and mobilized and when my stress is turned all the way up, what happens in my body?

What do I notice, and what do I not notice? What happens to my senses? What are the impulses I notice in my body?

Try noticing where energy is moving toward, away from, or building in your body, and feel it build, even for thirty seconds.

The color of this state is . . .

The sound of this state is . . .

The movement of this state is . . .

The picture of what this state feels like is . . .

The mobilization state often gets what it needs when we know we are safe and when we can move away from what is dangerous. Sometimes we are in danger now, and sometimes our bodies are remembering what was dangerous in the past and need help sensing that we are here now.

How can I tell the difference between when I am in danger now and when I am remembering what was dangerous in the past? (There are exercises later in this chapter designed specifically to help you work through the mobilization state.)

Shutting Down

When I start to shut down, what happens to my senses? What is happening in my body that tells me that I might begin to shut down? What kinds of thoughts do I have? What does the work around me seem like when I'm in a shut-down state?

When we feel ourselves shutting down, it can be difficult to know that there is hope, connection, or a way out of this state. Having tethers to other people, or to other feeling states, can remind us that we are not stuck here forever and that we do not have to be here alone.

What tethers remind you that you haven't always or won't always feel this way?

What person, memory, object, or being could join you in this place as long as you need to be here?

FOR WHEN WE ARE FEELING ACTIVATED

The following practices are designed to help us if we are experiencing activation, have been through trauma, or want to build resilience. Some might work well when you are somewhere on the stress-response staircase; others might help you feel more solid and sturdy when you are not experiencing activation.

Notice which practices feel useful right away, which ones come easily, and which ones seem to be more activating. Each of those responses is a useful piece of information that your body is communicating about who you are, where you've been, and what you need.

Boundary Skills

Try creating a circle around yourself using a string, rolled towels, or scarves. The circle represents a boundary from others' actions, thoughts, and feelings. Try experimenting with a circle that is as big as you want it to be or as close to your body as you can make it. Notice how it feels to have the boundary there, no matter its distance from you.

Try removing the visual representation of the boundary but allowing it to be there in your mind.

If someone is helping you with this exercise, have them come close to the boundary edge while still respecting the line. Experiment with moving the boundary closer to you or farther away.

Try placing your hands on your body somewhere that feels easy to make contact with. Notice where your hands end and where the part of you that you're touching begins. Sense what it is like to notice that this is a place where you exist, where you are contained within the boundary of your skin.

Try moving your hands over the surface of your body with a gentle pressure, missing no part of you and allowing this touch to help you feel the places you extend to, the outer edges of your self.

If you are practicing with a safe and trusted other, perhaps a partner or bodywork therapist, you might invite them to touch your body in agreed-upon ways and places. Notice the temperature of their touch, the pressure, how it feels to have a sense through their touch of where you end and where they begin.

Try pushing against a wall with two flat hands. Notice how different parts of your body feel as you practice pushing against something.

Try pushing with varying degrees of pressure, noticing which muscles in your hands, then arms, then back get activated.

Try using other body parts. Perhaps pushing with your back, seat, or shoulder, or with two flat feet while lying on the floor.

Try saying no with your whole body. Use a form or motion that captures the power and potency of a no in every part of your body but without needing to use words.

You might imagine something you find it easy to say no to. Imagine that situation, and practice communicating your full-body no.

Trying this in front of a mirror can be helpful as you see your body's language and how clear your communication can be.

If someone is around, you could ask them to prompt you with a question you might find it easy to say no to, whatever that is for you. And practice, over and over again, saying no with your whole body in a wordless way until it feels easy to do so.

Once you have done this, try thinking of something more difficult to say no to, and practice the exercise all over again.

For Comfort and Care

Give yourself a hug.

Rub your own shoulders, hands, or feet.

Wrap yourself in a blanket.

Make yourself a warm drink.

Put your hand on your heart and say, "I believe you, and I'm here with you now."

Breathing

Try developing a breathing practice. Pick a kind of breathing, and use it to start or end the day, to transition between tasks or parts of the day, to begin or end a meal, or to help you stay present in a difficult or enjoyable moment. Here are a few different types of breathing patterns:

Nasal breathing, where exhales extend longer than inhales

Breathing in, holding, breathing out, and holding (repeat), with each phase lasting five seconds

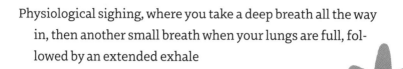

Physiological sighing, where you take a deep breath all the way in, then another small breath when your lungs are full, followed by an extended exhale

For Play and Expression

Put your hand on your heart and say, "I'm sorry you didn't get to play like this back then. We can do it together now."

Twirl around with a ribbon or a scarf in your hand.

Make silly faces into a mirror or take photos.

Play a game on your own or with others.

Put on music and dance. Try inviting the children in your life to join you, or dance along with them when they dance.

Try hopping on one foot or two feet.

Skip instead of walking somewhere.

Crawl on your hands and knees to get around your bedroom.

Try jumping on a bed.

Roll around, especially on a soft carpet, down a hill, or over grass.

For Nurturance and Presence

With your hands on your body, or touching an object or your environment to keep you present and grounded, try saying the following things:

You never have to go through that, exactly like that, again.

I'm here with you.

You are allowed to have feelings about what happened.

I will be with you as you feel the feelings.

I believe you.

It really did happen, it is over, and I'm here now.

I will stay with you as long as it takes.

We can be here, right now.

We can do this all together.

Thank you for trying to protect me with these reactions.

Thank you for telling the truth about just how scary and painful it was.

You are safe now.

What I know to be true about us now is . . .

For Release and Grounding

When experiencing activation in your body, you might notice racing thoughts, excess buzzing energy, tightness or tension in your muscles, feelings of being trapped or stuck, or feelings of reactivity or defensiveness. You may find it difficult to slow down, rest, and relax. Try the following in intervals, pausing in between to assess whether you want to keep going.

Run in place.

Notice your body's movements and keep doing them but in an exaggerated way.

Bounce your heels up and down on the ground.

Do jumping jacks.

Go for a walk or hike, climb stairs, or lift
weights.

Practice a physiological sigh.

Wiggle your whole body.

With your shoes off, put your feet in
water, walk on grass or soil, or stand
on sand or rocks.

Flop onto your bed.

Pretend to melt like an ice cube onto the
floor.

Wash your face with really cold water.

Have a whole-body tantrum for thirty
seconds.

ORIENTING PRACTICE

Notice the space around you as if you were going to re-create it in a painting. As you take a look around, try to slow the pace of your attention by half, really taking in everything. Look for colors, shapes, and textures that you feel drawn to or calmed by.

WHEN FEELING STRESS

If you need the stress in that moment, then try placing your hands on your body and saying, "Thank you for responding to help us get through whatever is going on. I know that you are doing everything you can to keep us safe."

If you do not need the stress in that moment, try placing your hands on your body and saying, "I'm so glad that you are there, helping me get ready for danger. Right now, I am safe, and I am going to take care of you. So you're welcome to step aside for now, and I am so relieved to know that you will be right there as soon as I need you to protect me."

When you feel calm, try making a voice recording on your phone of you saying these things out loud to listen to when you need to hear them.

I can learn to be safe with myself.

APPEARANCE and IMAGE

HOW WE SEE OUR BODY FROM THE OUTSIDE

When we talk about the body, it is normal to think about our image. Many of us have learned to see ourselves from the outside, as if our minds are hovering outside of ourselves. We've learned to imagine ourselves through the eyes of others, believing that how we look and what others think about our appearance are the most important parts of being a body. We come to see ourselves as objects that can be managed, evaluated, judged, or adored, forgetting that our bodies constitute ourselves and that our bodies include everything that lives inside our skin—all the systems that coordinate to help us feel, sense, heal cuts, remember, digest, smile, and sleep.

We can easily forget the rest of our bodies—especially if we learned that how we looked could get us or cost us love, safety, or connection—and prioritize our exterior. We can easily internalize the values we learn from those around us. These values are passed down through our caregivers, the media, and the people we spend time with, and they may come in the form of subtle, unspoken messages or clear, spoken communication.

It is easy to fixate on our image when we have had lots of practice doing so and when social reinforcement also encourages this fixation. But at some point, we realize this is costing us the fullness of who we are, from feeling present and at rest to enjoying our bodies to experiencing mental and physical health. The answer to being fixated on managing our image is to be more present in our bodies.

One way to do this is to practice *interoception*, which involves tapping into the senses that come from the inside of our bodies. Instead of living life on the outside looking in, we can learn to make a home inside our bodily selves through embodiment. We can become reacquainted with what lives under that image: our sensing, intuiting, pleasurable, feeling body.

WHAT MESSAGES WE RECEIVED

What messages did I hear growing up about my body? About bodies in general?

Where did those messages come from?

What was unsaid but communicated by my family about bodies? What was I told directly about what I should look like?

What pivotal moments do I remember from my youth that has shaped my thoughts and feelings about my image?

In the media I consumed growing up, what was considered a good body? What bodies were missing from the media I consumed? What about the media I consume now?

What are the parts of how I look that I find challenging to accept? When did that start? What would it be like if, without my body changing, I was able to accept my body as is?

What parts of my appearance am I learning to accept? When did I begin to accept these parts? How did that change begin? What does it feel like inside to notice the difference?

What parts of my appearance do I enjoy? What do I enjoy about them? What is it like to enjoy my body? When did I start to enjoy this part of my body in this way? What do I believe about myself when I enjoy this part of myself? What would happen if this was true about me, even if the rest of my body looked exactly as it looks?

MEETING OURSELVES WITH CARE

Try placing your hands on the parts of your body that you have judged or felt judgment for. As you let your hands linger there for a few moments, try bringing to mind someone you love. Feel kindness or warmth grow in your heart or in a smile on your face, and imagine that kindness could be directed through your fingers into the part of your body that you are touching. Allow it to flow in as long as you can tolerate.

Try looking at a part of your body in the mirror that you think is not ideal, that you think needs to be different, or that you feel shame about. Try saying the following:

I am so sorry we have learned you are not good enough.

You have never done anything wrong, even if the culture around us has forgotten that.

We are allowed to be here.

You are good.

I will work on healing so that you are safe with me, no matter what people around us say.

Or add your own statement here:

IF MY BODY WERE A HOUSE

If my body were a house, where would my sense of self usually live in relation to the house? Is it up in the attic, on the front lawn, or sprawled through the living room?

What makes it challenging to be inside the house? What makes it challenging to be outside the house?

What makes it feel good to be inside the house? What makes it feel good to be outside the house?

When did I leave the house? When do I leave the house now? How have I found my way back into the house?

What rooms inside the house are unfamiliar to me?

What inside rooms would I like to explore?

BEING NAKED

When time and privacy allow, try taking some or all of your clothes off and moving about your space as you typically would. Or you could dance, catching a glimpse of yourself in the mirror. Afterward, spend some time writing about your experience using the following prompts:

When I moved through my space without clothing, I was able to . . .

Without clothing, I noticed . . .

I appreciate that I can . . .

My naked body wants to say . . .

Sometimes, when we have had our bodily autonomy taken from us, it can feel difficult to have our clothing off. So if this exercise was short or not possible at this time, notice how it felt to put or keep your clothing on. What was it like to make this choice?

FINDING THE PULSE

Try to sense your heartbeat without taking your pulse.

This can take a long time to do, so if it does not happen right away, settle in and give yourself a few minutes to practice right now. Make a point of doing this regularly. You can also try sensing your heart rate by holding your breath when your lungs are full, by looking for a place your pulse is visible, or by doing thirty seconds of vigorous movement.

EMBODYING OURSELVES THROUGH NARRATIVE

As you read the following statements, try to go slowly. Notice what happens in your body. What is difficult? How do you know that? What might make it feel that way? What feels true or easy? How do you know that? What might contribute to it feeling that way?

My body is good, without conditions. The word "body" includes more than just appearance; it encompasses the fullness of what it means to be human.

I do not need to change my body in any way to be more valuable.

I do not need to punish myself for a changing appearance or for looking different at two points in time.

If it is hard to understand why my body is doing something, then I can assume there must be a reason, even if I don't know it now.

My appearance is a part of me, but it is not the only or most important part of me.

I can respond to negative thoughts about my body with curiosity and kindness, doing so to deepen self-trust and to create safety within myself.

My body is not bad, but cultural scripts have gotten many things wrong when it comes to bodies, and sometimes I get the two confused.

Instead of seeing my body as the problem (the medical/pathology model), I can see society's narrow definition of the ideal body as the problem (the social model).

Add your own statement here:

I AM AT HOME INSIDE MYSELF.

GETTING TO KNOW the EMOTIONAL BODY

Emotions are powerful, informative, and essential bodily processes. They are the energy that moves in co-ordinated ways through our bodies to help us stay safe, protected, and connected and to help us experience more of what makes life worth living. When we know how to notice that energy, allow it, make meaning of it, and manage it to suit our circumstances and present needs, our emotions help us be fully alive.

EACH FEELING MOVES IN OUR BODIES IN A PARTICULAR WAY AND HAS A SPECIFIC WAY OF HELPING US IN LIFE. There are many shades and combinations of feelings, but no matter what family we were born into or where we live in the world, we are all born with the following basic building blocks:

FEAR makes us alert, detects threat, and helps us get away from danger

SADNESS helps us encounter what is meaningful, signals we need care or rest, and helps us grieve

JOY helps us expand, heal, celebrate, connect, and share

DISGUST protects us from what is toxic to our bodily or social systems

EXCITEMENT gives us motivation, creates energy, and helps us explore and investigate

ANGER asserts, protects, defends, or helps us make change

DESIRE helps us get pleasure, identify wants, meet needs, and create

Feelings are both bodily and social, acting as sensory communication to us and to those around us. But not everyone knows how to respond in healthy and supportive ways to this form of communication. Growing up, we might have learned that some feelings were dangerous or untrustworthy, would cause us to be alone, or would create distress in others. We learned ways of expressing feelings that suited those around us, or we learned to defend against the feelings to protect ourselves and others from the pain of them.

But our unfelt feelings, like any other essential bodily processes, do not go away even if we try to repress them. They eventually catch up with us and get our attention somehow, sometimes in the form of disease, mental health issues, illness, burnout, addiction, or pain. To get back to our core self, the wise, creative, steady, compassionate, and connected present-day self, we need to learn to be with our feelings as they happen and to trust that our bodies know what to do with them, as long as our mental and cultural stories do not get in the way.

WHAT I LEARNED ABOUT FEELINGS

Growing up, the feelings I was allowed to feel were . . .

I learned that it would be dangerous to feel . . .

The feelings that I have learned to label as negative are . . .

I am afraid that if I feel _____ (fear, sadness, joy, disgust, excitement, anger, desire), then I might . . .

When I was little, I needed to learn that feelings . . .

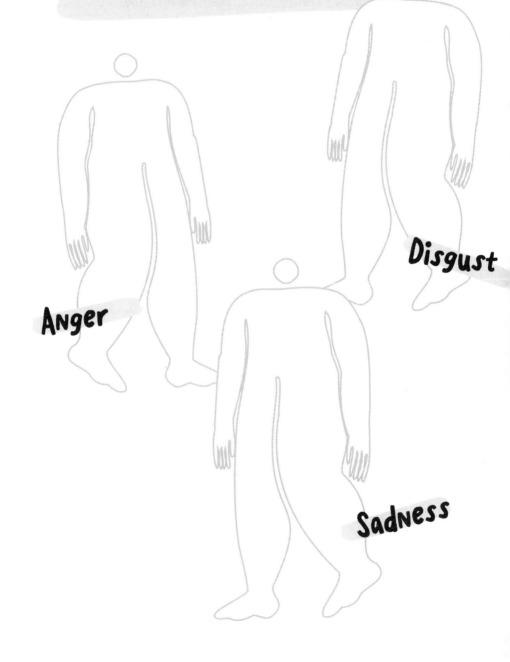

TENDING TO EACH EMOTION

On the body outline next to each emotion listed here, draw or shade where you feel the emotion in your body. If you are able, pick colors for each feeling.

Disgust

Anger

Sadness

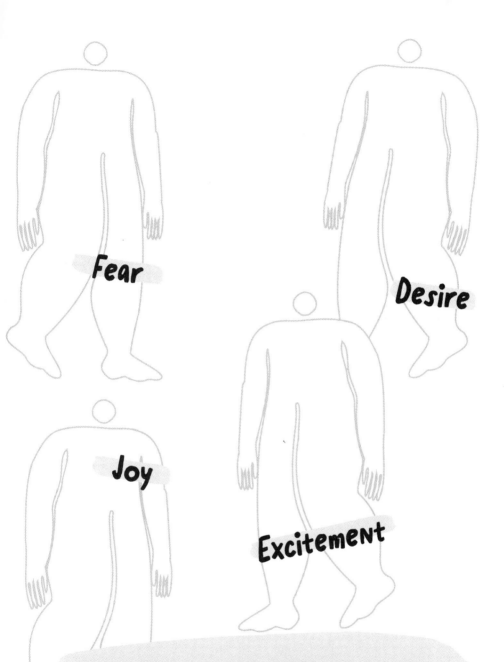

Fear

Desire

Joy

Excitement

For each of the seven emotions, reflect on the following:

What do you need to know to trust this feeling?

What do you need to tolerate this feeling a little more?

Complete this sentence: "The way I get away from this feeling is . . ."

Complete this sentence: "The shape this feeling wants to make is . . ."

GETTING BACK TO CORE EMOTIONS

The Triangle of Experience

We leave our core feelings by moving into our inhibitory emotions or our defenses. According to psychodynamic psychotherapies, to get back to our core state, we need to find our way back to our core feelings, and we need to stay with them until we get through to the other side. [1]

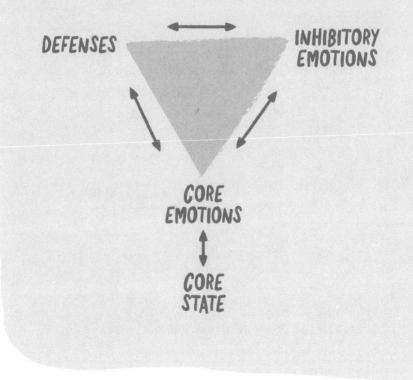

DEFENSES

INHIBITORY EMOTIONS

CORE EMOTIONS

CORE STATE

Emotions: fear, sadness, joy, disgust, excitement, anger, desire

Inhibitory emotions: shame, guilt, anxiety

Defenses: denial, avoidance, talking over, minimizing, numbing, self-harm, intellectualizing, humor, ignoring, changing the subject, averting one's gaze, smiling or laughing, withdrawing, vagueness, projection, substance use, intimidation, mockery, judgment, blaming, aggression, violence, eating, masturbation, people pleasing, and so on. (*Note*: We know something is a defense if it is being used to escape our inner experience or core emotion rather than express a core emotion.)

At what point on the triangle do you find yourself right now?

What defenses jump out to you?

Accessing Your Core State

Remember a time you felt curious, connected, or courageous. If you can, try to bring more memories of feeling this way to mind, including memories that feel calm, creative, or compassionate. You could also think of a person you care about or feel calm around or connected to. As you bring all of this to mind, notice what you feel in your body. You might notice feeling a weight to your body, feeling steady internally. Or you might notice that it's quieter in your mind, and you might feel that your spine is upright but relaxed.

What is a word, object, or color that represents this state?

Imagine that the word, object, or color you chose lives somewhere inside your core between your pelvis and your throat. Spend a few minutes letting it really sink in, making space for it to be here, soaking it in.

When you are in this state, try smelling a particular smell, imagining that this sensation could be infused with the smell. In the future, when you feel the need to access this state, try smelling the same smell.

Exercises for All Points on the Triangle

Put on a song and dance from the place of your core state, using your body like a paintbrush to bring the color of your core self into the space around you.

Write a letter to the defense(s) you rely on most. If you are able to, thank it for how it has helped you and protected you, and give it some updated information on what you believe about feelings now. Try asking the defense a question and listen to how it responds.

Feelings as bodily sensations are different from the ruminative and unhelpful thoughts about ourselves that we associate with them. When you are feeling, try to stay as much with the sensations as possible. Instead of thinking, *I am alone, and I will be that way forever*, you might try thinking, *I am feeling such deep sadness, and I wish someone could be with me in this place. It is scary to be here without someone to reassure me of how long it will take to get to the other side.*

Who is the person you could trust to stay with you during the feelings you have? They could be real, imaginary, historical, familiar to you, or someone you've only heard of. Imagine they are next to you right now, looking into your eyes or putting their hand on your shoulder. What would they say? How does it feel inside to imagine being near them?

WAVES OF EMOTIONS

DEFENSES

RELIEF AND INSIGHT

Emotions come like waves: a sensation rises, peaks with intensity, and then softens down the other side. As emotions rise, we may have learned to use our defenses to protect us from pain or fear of the feeling. But when we stay with the feeling, on the other side is where we find insight about what to do next and where we feel relief and connection to ourselves.

Where else in nature, life, or my body, do I see the form of waves?

What can those patterns teach me about tolerating and staying with emotions?

TOLERATING UNCOMFORTABLE FEELINGS

To increase our tolerance of uncomfortable feelings, we can practice building our tolerance of other kinds of discomfort. You could try a different one each day for a week, or you could do the same practice every day for a week.

Try doing a simple task with your nondominant hand instead of your dominant hand.

Move in a way that is twice as slow as you normally would for a few minutes.

Try changing your level at an unexpected time: do what you are doing on your tip toes or crouched down.

Pick a stretch and hold it a little bit longer than you are used to.

Put a tissue or cotton ball under your foot in your sock.

Take a bath or shower that is slightly hotter or cooler than feels natural.

Try to use space differently, sprawling if you prefer to curl in or pulling yourself inward if you are used to stretching out.

You are
GOOD.
You have
ALWAYS
been
GOOD.

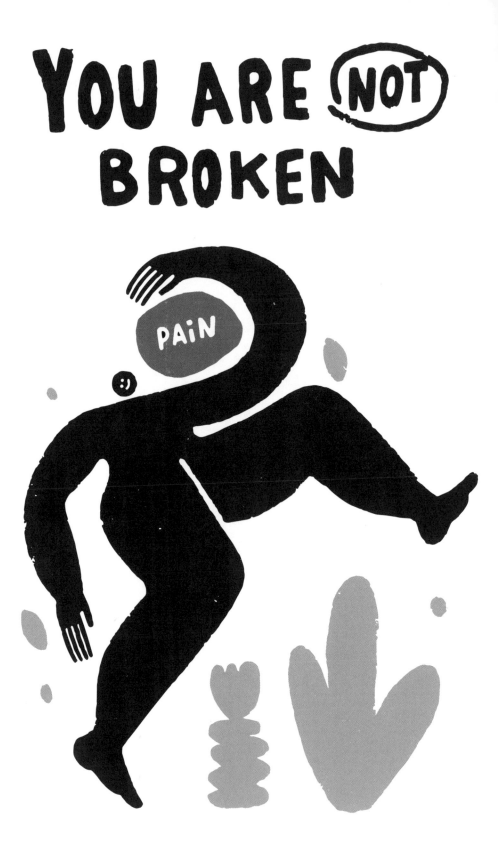

RELATiNG DiFFERENTLY to PAiN, iLLNESS, and iNJURY

Pain, illness, and injury can force our attention back into our bodies in an uncomfortable way, disrupting our dis-embodied ideas of ourselves. When we have learned to escape into our minds as a way of getting far from the complexity and

challenge of being a body, pain, illness, and injury can seem like the proof that we should not have been in our bodies all along. They can be proof of our bodily failure, unless we take a wider perspective and see our mistrust for our changing, needy, vulnerable, and impermanent bodies as a failure of the social systems that we exist in. Taking this wider view allows us to begin to see that there is not and has never been anything wrong with our bodies, only the stories we were told about them and the systems built around those stories. Pain, illness, and injury can become invitations to listen to our bodily selves, to accept nurturance, to turn toward what hurts without ignoring what also feels good, and to experiment with our interdependence. Nothing will teach us more about the limits of our self-sufficient values than being unable to do what we used to do easily.

(*Note*: We all struggle with different things. If the word "pain" does not resonate with you or if another word is more suitable, feel free to substitute it with something that works better.)

BELIEFS ABOUT PAIN

What are my beliefs about bodies that are in pain, sick, or injured?

Where did I inherit those beliefs?

How has it served me to believe those things?

What is the cost, and to whom, of the stories I believe about bodies in illness, pain, or injury?

FIRST AND SECOND ARROWS

Life shoots the first arrow: we experience the pain of being human.

We shoot the second arrow: we add to the pain by what we say, think, and feel about our human experience.

What are the first arrows I have experienced?

What does my second arrow look and sound like?

When we experience human pain, confusing life experiences that surprise us or leave us feeling out of control, we often blame ourselves. This self-blame plays many roles: (1) It helps us feel in control and make sense of pain in a rudimentary way; (2) it is what we learned to do; we heard it happen and it stuck; and (3) it can help us feel motivated to change, for a while.

It is often easier to blame ourselves, or others, than it is to feel the feelings of fear or sadness that are underneath the blame.

Complete the following sentences:

"I blame myself in order to . . ."

"When I blame myself, then . . ."

There are several ways to explain the connection between our inner worlds, our life circumstances, and the pain we feel. One of them is the fear→tension→pain cycle that connects our unprocessed emotions (which show up as tightness) and the resulting pain we feel. Another one is the tightness→pain→second-arrow cycle, where we feel pain because of the tightness in our bodies, but then we add more pain by how we respond to the bodily experience we are having.

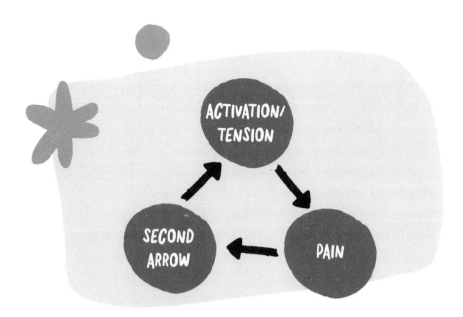

What would it be like to set the second arrow down and to add nurturance to the pain?

What can I do when I feel pain, need rest, or experience illness? What feels like nurturance for me?

It is normal for us to want to avoid the things that are painful or difficult to be with, especially if we are afraid to turn toward them, afraid they might swallow us whole. Ironically, it is when we learn to be with our pain or the difficult experiences that we bring in the nurturance we need and avoid adding more pain to what we are already carrying.

Think of someone you love, and imagine if they were to experience the same first arrow that you are experiencing. What would you say to them to bring them comfort?

Imagine saying that to yourself, or try writing a letter to them about that experience, offering care, support, and validation, but instead of putting their name at the top, put your own.

GREETING YOUR PAIN

Imagine you are on a park bench, and you are showing up as your core self—the wise, loving, curious one we met in an earlier exercise. Coming toward you is your pain (or illness or injury).

How does it look? How does it move? How do you feel, from the place of your core self, as pain approaches you?

You see yourself welcome pain, inviting it to sit next to you.

Start by thanking it for being there and mending the rift between you. You might say something like, "I am so glad you are here. We are often together, but I haven't really made much time to get to know you, and I'm sorry for that. I want to know you better and build trust between us."

Then ask it a question, from that kind, curious place inside. Try to get to know it like you would try to get to know anyone else who was important but misunderstood.

No matter where you get to in the end, thank it for coming and make a point to connect with it again like this soon.

CHANGING THE PAIN CYCLE

Instead of going through the second-arrow pain cycle, try the following next time you experience fear, pain, or tension to build trust with yourself:

Observe the emotional and physical reactions. Don't judge them, just notice them.
Respond with kindness and curiosity.
Notice what happens next; watch for signs of softness and release.

LEARNING THE SKILL OF FEELING PLEASURE

When we have been in pain for a long time, we may need to learn the skill of feeling pleasure or neutrality. This may be difficult at first, but keep practicing.

Scan your body in search of something that feels neutral or positive. Let your attention wander inside and outside your body, noticing things like temperature, posture, texture, satiety, contact with your environment, or anything that you might not notice often because they feel neutral—like nailbeds, earlobes, or eyelids.

Make a list in your mind, collecting a few places that feel pleasurable or neutral and letting your mind linger there as long as possible, returning back to those places when you feel distracted.

Ask those places in your body what they want to say; imagine they have a voice and can speak to you.

Ask if those places in your body have something to offer the places of pain. Those places may not have words, but you may imagine a color or a pattern of energy moving between these two places. See what happens next.

Thank those parts of your body for being there.

PRESENT WITH PAIN

Try doing something intentional that creates minor discomfort: make a stretch, hold an ice cube, or pinch your palm. As you notice the sensation of discomfort or pain, try practicing the voice of the inner nurturer, perhaps saying to yourself, "I'm here with you in this" each time you experience the unpleasurable sensation.

Write a love poem to your pain.

Put on a song and dance with your pain, inviting it to come with you as you move.

I am so sorry it has been so difficult. I am listening, and I want to know about how it hurts. I want to be here through it all. You can tell the story as long as you need to.

The Body and Oppression

WHEN BODIES ARE (POLITICAL)

Social power is communicated about and through bodies and the artificial lines drawn by people who are conferred the most social power. This creates binary categories where people find themselves on one side of the made-up line: acceptable or unacceptable, valued or feared, normal or abnormal. No matter what we were told or shown, no body is better or more deserving of respect and consideration than any other body. When we can begin to reclaim the parts of our body that have been disavowed by the systems that cause fragmentation, we can remember ourselves as whole, and we can begin to build systems that support the development and flourishing of whole people.

The construction of power and oppression is not only about bodies; it also impacts our lived realities. It fuels the stress we experience trying to navigate systems that were not designed for our bodies, the ongoing burden of facing certain kinds of danger, and the fear and grief we feel when the impact of these lived realities are denied or invisible. When we have accepted the way our culture speaks about our bodies, it can be difficult to see how this hierarchy exists and impacts us. This can include the places where we are socially devalued, but it is especially true of the places in our lives where we have the most social power.

Too often when it comes to bodies, *power* and *normal* are conflated. But when we change our definition of power, we can see that something better and more beautiful can be created. There is an opportunity for real connection, the kind that dissolves these bodily hierarchies, when we make space for pain to be witnessed and validated, tolerate our fear and recognize our defenses against change, learn to see how our bodies give us easy access to social spaces, learn from those whose experiences are different from ours, and make room to rest, play, and create in the midst of it all.

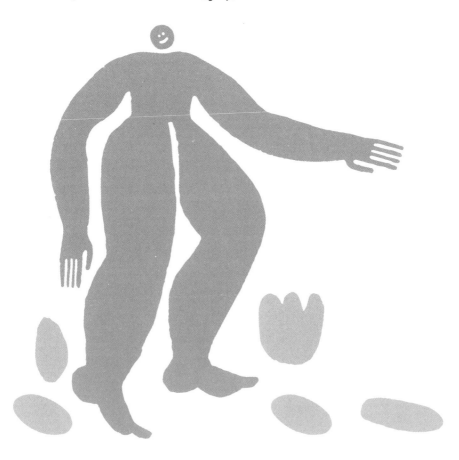

MY BODY AND POWER

How have I experienced power because of my body?

What does that feel like?

How have I felt devalued because of my body?

What does that feel like?

When I hold both of these realities inside at the same time, what emotions, sensations, impulses, and thoughts emerge?

Anger, guilt, shame, and fear are often featured in conversations about oppression and the body. When does my anger show up? When does my guilt emerge? What does shame try to help with? What about this topic or conversation am I afraid of? It may be useful to try to answer these questions two or three times, asking yourself, "And what else, and what else, and what else?"

When I am having conversations about oppression, power, and bodily hierarchies, I notice my defenses show up as these sensations, emotions, and thoughts:

When I notice myself getting defensive, it will help me to . . .

FINDING SAFETY

In conversations about oppression, the language of "being safe" and "safety" often comes up without us thinking about what it actually means. When you think of the word "safe," what comes to mind? Remember a time you felt socially and emotionally safe. What was happening then? What did it feel like inside your body?

Take a form or make a gesture for what safety feel likes.

Other words for "safe" are . . .

Safety is like . . .

To help others feel this way, I need to be able to . . .

BRINGING CONNECTION TO WHERE IT HURTS

Call up your core self, the one we worked on developing in the chapter "Feeling Feelings." When you have a sense of your core self as a bodily experience, remember a time you were without social power or were put on the margins. Imagine you could go to that younger version of yourself and nurture and care for them. Ask them to show you where it hurt. Ask them to show you what that was like. Ask them what they would have needed from you if you were there. Imagine yourself giving that to them, and if you're able, invite this younger self into the present, to live inside of you instead of back in that memory.

Try accessing a similar memory, but this time, instead of bringing yourself in, bring in all the other people who know what this feeling is like. Allow yourself to take in their presence, seeing them around you and hearing their comments. Notice what this is like.

With your core self alive inside of you, notice what your curiosity and courage feel like. Take a form for what it feels like to be curious and courageous. Imagine bringing this self into your next challenging situation or conversation, especially with someone whom you perceive to be different from you.

Rather than responding as I have in the past, engaging with someone from this place allows me to . . .

MOVEMENTS FOR CHANGE

Take a form or movement for what it has been like to have social power.

Take a form or movement for what it has been like to be without social power.

Take a form or movement for what you want power to look and feel like.

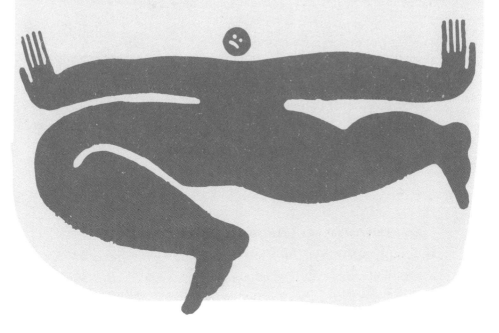

Bring to mind a social script in which you have participated in some way—a story about which bodies are valuable, which bodies are dangerous, or who you need to be to have power in this culture. Walk around the room in a way that captures how it feels to be in that social script. Then, with that same social script in mind, try walking for a minute in each of these ways:

In a playful way
In a curious way
In an angry way
Differently than anyone expects
As your core self

Bring to mind a difficult situation that might otherwise have you feeling frozen, angry, or scared. While holding that situation in your mind, try the following practices. Notice what happens to how you think and feel about the situation.

Wiggle or shake your whole body
Open your hands and look ahead
Bare your teeth
Slow down and take five deep physiological sighs
Stretch
Get up, walk around, and then sit back down
Place your hands on your belly and heart
Dance

No matter what has been said about your body, there is a knowing inside that you are valuable and deserve to be here. Try moving your awareness through your body, from head to toe, and ask your body to reveal where this knowing lives.

When I experience the value of MY BODY, I want to create a world that protects the value of YOUR BODY.

AND ENJOYMENT

THE SENSUAL and SEXUAL BODY

Our sexuality is central to our embodied experience of life.
Unlike what we were likely taught, sexuality is not constrained
to our genitals or to our sexual behavior with a specific other.
And even if we were told otherwise, it does not belong to someone else. It is the ineffable quality of wanting that drives us
toward closeness, fulfillment, self-expression, and pleasure in
all its forms. Our sexuality is ours, belongs to us, and is for us. It

is connected to our power, our senses of knowing, and our longings for wholeness. It is here in you right now, moving through you even as you read this.

Based on the constraints imposed on our ideas of sexuality, exploring our relationships to it in the present can feel challenging, scary, or shameful. Other times, it can feel exhilarating. Sometimes it feels like both at the same time. As you work

FIVE CIRCLES OF SEXUALITY

Dennis Dailey's five circles of sexuality model proposes that sexuality invites us into a more holistic perspective of our sexual selves.[2] The five circles include power and sexualization, sensuality, sexual health and reproduction, intimacy, and sexual identity.

Try using the following figure as a mind or image map. Write or name aloud what comes to mind as you encounter each circle. If you have had significant shifts in the sense of your sexuality, try doing this twice, once for the you prior to these shifts and once for the present you.

Notice which circles are most difficult for you to interact with.

through the exercises in this chapter, I invite you to reflect on the multiplicity of experiences you have when exploring your sexuality. Draw on the exercises from past chapters involving the second arrow, tolerating emotion, and the importance of curiosity.

SEXUAL IDENTITY — labels we use for who and what we desire

SENSUALITY — how we use our senses to experience pleasure

INTIMACY — closeness between us and anyone we love in any way or form

POWER AND SEXUALIZATION — positive and negative exchanges of power through sexuality based on social and political context

SEXUAL HEALTH AND REPRODUCTION — body parts and their function for sexual expression and childbearing

"Sharing of joy, whether physical, emotional, psychic, or intellectual, forms a bridge between the sharers which can be the basis for understanding much of what is not shared between [people], and lessens the threat of their difference . . . and can give us the energy to pursue genuine change within the world."

—Audre Lorde[3]

Make a list of what brings you pleasure in any form. Don't forget to include people, food, places, sounds, and activities.

Write the story of your sexual identity, whatever that means to you.

Intimacy includes trust, risk, vulnerability, emotional connection, and the quality of being seen, known, and cherished.

Complete the following sentences:
"My history with intimacy can be described as . . ."

"When it comes to intimacy, what I want for myself is . . ."

Make a movement or take a posture that expresses the following:

Sensuality	Desire
Sexuality	Pleasure
Connection	

Take a moment to reflect on how those postures were similar or different and what you make of that.

MOVEMENT AND MUSIC

Try putting on some music and inviting your sensual self to dance with you. If you are not sure where to start, try playing with movement in your hips and slowing down the pace you would typically move at.

Next, put on a song that allows you to connect with your erotic self. Try to keep your hands moving across your body for the duration of the song.

Put on music and dance in front of the mirror, not breaking eye contact with yourself.

WITH A PARTNER

If you have a consenting partner, try trading hand massages a few times. If possible, try setting the timer for at least three minutes. When you are receiving the hand massage, first try to simply receive it. Let your hands be touched, and notice what feels good. Take turns offering the same experience to your partner. On the next round, try telling them exactly how you would like them to massage your hand. Take note of pressure, location, pace, and types of touch. Take turns offering your partner the same experience.

WHEN YOU'RE ALONE

When you have privacy and time allows, try touching your own body and experimenting with what kinds of touch feel pleasurable.

Where do you want to let your hands linger?

What parts of your own body do you forget to touch?

As you engage with this exercise, try to notice your emotions, temperature, thoughts, memories, and sense of presence. If you notice that it is difficult to stay with your own touch in the present, try one of the grounding exercises from "The Body Overwhelmed" chapter, pausing to bring your attention back into the present moment and either taking a break or continuing with your self-exploration.

Try holding yourself with your hands on your face, neck, or around your body. Pause to press your fingers gently into your skin, noticing the sensation of your own touch. Hold yourself the way you would hold someone you love, imagining that kind of care drifting out your fingers and into your own skin and then traveling through your body and out your fingers again. Try to notice the unbroken line of connection you are holding within yourself right now.

WHAT WANTING FEELS LIKE

Our bodies contain action impulses connected to what we feel drawn toward and what we want to get away from. Our wanting moves through our body as an approach tendency, which means we lean forward. Our dislike moves through our body as a withdrawal or avoidance tendency, which means we lean away or turn away. We can encounter our wanting by listening to our body's subtle movements and impulses. Try thinking of something you know you really want, and sense the draw forward. Do the same exercise with something you really do not want, noticing anything that feels like it's pulling your head, neck, feet, core, or shoulders away. Try this exercise again with something you are not sure if you want or not, like when standing in front of the fridge trying to decide on a snack.

Try placing a single hand gently on your genitals, and imagine directing gratitude toward them. Thank them for what they have done and for what they have helped you experience. Apologize to them for what they have endured that they should not have had to, and ask them if they would like to tell you more about what they want and need now.

During an orgasm, try to notice where in your body the sensation begins, what color it has, and where the energy ends. Try to experience it as it is happening in such a way that you could describe it to someone who has never had the experience.

What other forms of sexual expression are satisfying for you besides orgasm? Besides orgasm, what other experiences make a sexual encounter with another feel valuable and worth pursuing?

Try making a form, shape, movement, sound, posture, or gesture for what orgasm is like for you.

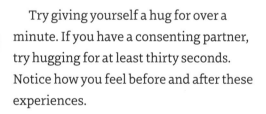

Try giving yourself a hug for over a minute. If you have a consenting partner, try hugging for at least thirty seconds. Notice how you feel before and after these experiences.

PLEASURE EXCHANGE

Try asking someone close to you about what brings them pleasure.

Try asking that same person if they would be open to a pleasure exchange: intentionally offering each other something in the coming days that brings the other person joy and delight. This could be sensual or touch based, or it could be something like getting a favorite coffee, making a special meal, or going on a walk together to a beautiful place.

MY PLEASURE is my birth-right and an essential part of being A BODY.

RECONCILING the (SPIRIT) AND <u>BODY</u> DIVIDE

Spirituality is a person's wired-in longing for a sense of interconnectedness and the Sacred. Our cultural landscape is permeated by inherited philosophical and theological paradigms urging us to control and disavow our bodies to get away from what is dangerous about being human as a means of getting closer to what is sacred. This way of thinking has been the justification for disembodiment for millennia on the grounds that our bodies are here but what is divine is only elsewhere and outside of our human experience and the material world—this is the idea of *transcendence*. The invitation of *immanence* is to bring our awareness to how the sacred is here and now, permeating matter, moving through and within us as bodies and moving through and within all matter. This helps us see that our bodies are not obstacles to our spirituality but are the doorway into sensing, experiencing, and feeling how the Sacred is within and between us.

The Greek word for "spirit," *pneuma*, can be translated as "breath" or "breathed," like the breath that is alive in you right now or the way our bodies breathe themselves. When we begin to look to the here and now to find what is sacred, we can be in the fullness of our lives in the present instead of waiting for real life to begin later. When the body-spirit divide begins to heal, we grow in being able to attune to our own bodies, how we tend to and honor the earth, and how we relate to those we were told were "other." This is the beginning of learning to see that the Holy has always been precisely in the places we were told not to look.

What am I connected to, right now, through my senses?

Who and what am I connected to, as a body, in the past, present, and future?

My body is made of rhythms, just like the earth is made of rhythms. When I remember that I am like the earth, then . . .

Make yourself a snack, and before you eat, try to think of each item that makes up the food in front of you: Where did it come from? Who helped to make it? And what processes were involved? Who tended the land to grow the ingredients? Bring these people to mind as you eat, and if you are able, imagine thanking them.

OUR BODIES IN SEASON

Complete the following sentences:

"If fall was a form or a movement or a sound, it would be . . ."

"Fall teaches me that being a body . . ."

"In fall, my body is like the earth in that . . ."

"The feelings I have in fall are . . ."

"If winter was a form or a movement or a sound, it would be . . ."

"Winter teaches me that being a body . . ."

"In winter, my body is like the earth in that . . ."

"The feelings I have in winter are . . ."

"If spring was a form or a movement or a sound, it would be . . ."

"Spring teaches me that being a body . . ."

"In spring, my body is like the earth in that . . ."

"The feelings I have in spring are . . ."

"If summer was a form or a movement or a sound, it would be . . ."

"Summer teaches me that being a body . . ."

"In summer, my body is like the earth in that . . ."

"The feelings I have in summer are . . ."

THE LAND WE STAND ON

Try putting your bare feet on the ground.
You can do this anywhere, but it's ideal to do it where you live and to think of the history of that land. The land you are standing on is a place where people lived, died, held ceremonies, tended to their young, made love, felt grief, and saw visions. This land was known intimately by the people who lived on it long before we got here, and they knew how to honor it. Hold the living relationship with the land in your mind, and if you are able, communicate to it your appreciation, awe, and gratitude. Imagine sending appreciation, awe, and gratitude to the people whose land you live on.

Allow your body to settle into a posture that feels right for you to be in for a while. Allow yourself to bring your attention to your breathing, really noticing the quality of your inhale and your exhale for a few rounds of breath. As you breath out, allow yourself to notice how your body naturally supports you to let go of what it cannot hold anymore. On your next few exhales, think of what you are trying to let go or what you want help letting go of. As you breathe in, allow yourself to notice how your body naturally supports you to take in what you need. On your next few breaths, think of what you need or what you want to take in, and imagine that coming into you as you inhale.

Bring your attention to the whole cycle of breathing, the unending cycle of in and out that your body knows how to do.

BREATHING AND MOVING WITH THE MOON

As you create space to focus on your breath, imagine dividing up your breath into four sections that parallel the phases of the moon. The inhale is like the waxing of the moon. The pause at the top of your breath when your lungs are full is like the full moon. The exhale is like the waning of the moon. And the pause between when your lungs are empty and when you breathe again is like the new moon. Try to give your attention to each phase of the breath, allowing yourself to notice it as a distinct portion of the whole. As you travel through this cycle, notice which one you feel drawn to right now: waxing, full, waning, or new. Give that portion of your breath some special attention for the next few rounds. Perhaps even ask that portion of your breath, "What do you want me to know? What is it about this that I need something from right now?"

As you end, bring your awareness back to the full cycle of each four sections of breath, sensing it as a whole.

✱ **Try the same exercise with movement or form. Make a gesture or take a form or movement that represents the full moon—the fullest version of the light.** Travel as a body toward what feels smaller and newer, pausing in a form that represents the new moon. Then travel as a body again toward the form that represents the full moon.

As you engage in this cycle a few times, notice which of the four sections of movement you feel drawn to: waxing, full, waning, or new. And as you continue your movements, ask yourself, "What is it about this that is drawing me in?" Ask the movement, this phase of the cycle, and your body if they have something that you need to explore. You might do this by elongating this section of the movement, by adding more movement, by changing how much space you give the movement, or by adding a sound or words. As you explore this section of the cycle, return to your original two forms or movements and the transition between them. Place your hands on your body and thank yourself for this gift of exploration, time, and space.

EMBODIED PRAYERS

I used to think of prayer as asking the Creator for something mostly using my mind. But I have started to think about prayer differently by imagining it as a way to express what is inside of me with honesty and believing my Creator witnesses that, and by practicing living into what it is that I want. This naturally makes me wonder about how to pray with my body. No matter what your relationship with prayer or the Sacred is, I invite you to use these embodied prayers to practice creating with your body, symbolically, the kind of world that you want to inhabit. In doing this, praying is not just about asking for things outside of us but about practicing letting ourselves be changed into more whole versions of ourselves, trusting that when we are more whole, we build a world where others are welcomed into more of their wholeness.

For this practice, take the form suggested, or something like it, and think or say the words that go along with it.

Hands open to the sides or in front: "I remember that I am both always giving and always receiving. What do you have to offer me? What are you asking me to offer up?"

Holding self with arms: "From the moment I was created, I have been known, loved, and held. May I learn to receive this love and, out of the overflow, offer it to others."

Getting wide and tall: "It is through love that I expand, grow, and develop. Remind me that I am called to restore structures that inhibit this for others and that my expanding is always tied to the expanding of others."

Getting into a tiny ball: "Even in my smallness, I am not alone. Making myself small reminds me to remember those I have made small and to grieve with those who have been told that their bodies need to disappear."

Standing up: "It's through love that I rise and move. I am joining in the rising of my community, and I see that as the same as my own rising."

Resting head in hands: "Thank you for the body that needs rest, that reminds me to not always be doing so much, and that urges me to give up my attachment to productivity."

Rubbing neck, shoulders, and face: "Through my body I experience and express comfort. Through my body I can be the hands of gentleness and compassion for myself and for those around me."

Breathing intentionally: "I am thankful for this breath, the in and out reminding me that we are made of cycles—in our individual bodies and as a collective body—and that we live in relationship with the body of the earth. I am reminded that we are always changing and that cycles are part of our design."

After trying these practices, try some embodied prayers of your own. What is something you want to remember, live into, and invite into the world? What is a form or movement that represents that? What is a form or movement that feels important, and what words come out of that place for you?

MY BODY IS A LANDSCAPE OF INTERCONNECTION.

CONCLUSION

Practices to Return to Ourselves

Being a body is a wonderful, mysterious thing in that our bodily selves are our home, but they are also constantly changing. They are fully and completely ours, and they are the doorway to connection with all other life. Perhaps you will continue to integrate some of the experiences in this book into your life, and perhaps you will return to some that land differently when you are in a different season.

Take time to reflect on what stirred something or settled something. What you are yearning for will tell you so much about who you are. The more you know about who you are, the better you can meet your needs, ask for help, articulate your boundaries, care for yourself, and listen to the nudges inside that tell you about what comes next and who you are becoming.

Through the exercises in this book, how has your experience of embodiment changed? When did that happen? What was it like? How does it feel inside to remember that?

What exercises will you return to? What exercises didn't quite land for you? What meaning do you make of that?

If you could travel back to a younger version of yourself who needed to know some of this, who would you go visit, and what would you tell them? What happens inside of you as you reflect on this?

Complete the following sentences:

"My relationship with my body is . . ."

"I am grateful my body can . . ."

"When my mind and my body are friends, then . . ."

"I want . . ."

"Right now I can feel . . ."

"My body deserves nurturance in the form of . . ."

"The next step is . . ."

APPENDIX

A Leader's Guide

Our bodies are places of connection to ourselves, to each other, and to the world around us. As a book about experiencing embodiment, this book is meant to be lived, felt, experimented with, and used as a tool for connection. In what follows, I offer some suggestions about how to integrate the exercises into groups you are already part of or how to build a group specifically around these exercises.

Setting

If you have a group you are part of, or if you are thinking about starting a group for the purpose of doing these exercises together, pay attention to space. How our bodies encounter space impacts our felt sense of ourselves. Try to select a space that is accessible for a variety of bodies, and have available any mobility aids people might need. Pay attention to chair sizes, having options for different sizes of bodies. Things like lighting, background noise, and privacy of the space all impact how much we might like to try new things or how exposed we might feel during the process.

Ideally, find a meeting location where there are comfortable places to sit that can accommodate various body sizes and shapes and where people can arrange themselves in a circle. Having enough space to get up and move, clear access to exits, and easily movable chairs will help participants feel like the space is supporting them, rather than them having to adapt their expressions and experiments to the space. If participants are new to the space, then before the group starts, be sure to give them a description or a photo and include a description of accessibility so that people feel informed and prepared. Knowing about the space we are about to enter can help our bodies feel more at ease, which allows us to focus on the activities at hand.

Preparation

When using the exercises with a group, let participants know if they will need special equipment or if they will be invited to move in a way that is outside of what they might be expecting. If people will need clothes to move freely in, a journal, or a snack, make sure to give them enough notice to prepare ahead of time. If the exercises require music, make sure that you have songs picked out ahead of time. Make sure you have good speakers, and check the sound levels before your group starts.

Your own preparation counts too. If you are leading an exercise, try it a few times on your own, perhaps even recording yourself and watching the recording, to see how the exercise feels and to get comfortable with the language or any adaptations you might want to make. If you know that people with disabilities are engaging in the exercises and you are planning to make adaptations so they can participate, think about that ahead of time so you have suitable alternatives ready to present to the whole group. However, no matter your assumption of homogeneity in the group, providing options for the exercises is a great way to empower people to feel bodily autonomy or agency.

Intentionally selecting activities can make the experience more meaningful. If your group is meeting to discuss spirituality, trying practices in the "Holy Flesh" chapter might feel like a better fit than the exercises in the "Appearance and Image" chapter. That said, including exercises specifically designed to invite participants into a new experience of themselves can be particularly useful if there is time to reflect and share about the experiences and to integrate the experiences into their understanding of themselves and their connection to the group.

Group Design

If you are running a group specifically designed to work through the content of this book, here are some ideas:

You could meet for approximately ten weeks and work through one chapter each week. You could read the beginning of the chapter together at the beginning of gatherings, then pick a few exercises to try together, leaving time after each exercise to reflect, share, write, or be silent.

You could meet for approximately nine weeks. After each participant reads the book in its entirety, have a different person lead each week, sharing about what their experiences were like and selecting exercises that resonated with them the most.

You could meet at regular intervals throughout the year, perhaps as the seasons change, on the full moon, or around significant cultural holidays. You could try the same exercises each time, allowing yourself to develop a ritual or practice with each exercise and noticing how they feel different each time you do them, even though the exercises are the same.

If you are meeting with a book club to read *The Wisdom of Your Body*, you could use the exercises in this book that coordinate with corresponding chapters. Have group members read a chapter each week, and when you meet, practice selected exercises to deepen your experiences of the content.

Process

When meeting as a group, the following strategies can help your group be as effective and therapeutic as possible.

Spend time during the first meeting being clear about group expectations. Talking about this helps people know what they are responsible for, and it creates clarity about how members can build a group that feels respectful and enjoyable. Include things like attire, timing, lateness, communication between groups, payment, eating or food, how to listen and respond nonjudgmentally, advice-giving or active listening, and meeting preparation.

Try to start each meeting with a check-in or check-out. Avoid lengthy stories; instead, have people name their emotions or sensations or share something meaningful that the group needs to know about what they have been going through. Start and end the meeting the same way each time to create a sense of predictability and continuity.

Have leaders also participate in the exercises. Instead of observing, join in with others. Invite others to come to you for support or to interrupt you if they need help with something.

Use invitational language. Encourage people to make choices about what they will and will not participate in. Create a culture of agency and nonjudgment where people are allowed to decide what works for them, including adapting exercises on their own or as a group. Frame the activities in terms of exercises or experiences. The activities are not something to accomplish or succeed at but a place we can go to meet ourselves.

Set specific time boundaries for the group, and do your best to stick to them. If you have to go longer than the allotted time, notice that as soon as possible. Then let people know that the meeting might run long and give those who need to leave the permission to do so. Honoring time boundaries is more likely to happen if you plan ahead and estimate how long each activity might take. During the meeting, give participants guidance about how much or how little you want them to share when you ask open-ended questions. For example, say something like, "Let us know in a sentence or two . . ." or "We have time for each of you to share for five minutes."

Invite feedback at the end of each meeting or between meetings. Waiting until the end to ask for feedback makes it difficult to adapt the group to suit the needs of the participants. When people offer feedback, it can sometimes be difficult to assess if the feedback is something they are asking to change or a reflection of the person's experiences and preferences. It can be helpful to have an objective and trusted friend who has experience working with groups. Talking through feedback with this person can help you assess what to do with it and how much needs to change, if anything. Thank people for giving you feedback, no matter what it is: sharing how they are experiencing something with someone who is in a position of power is risky and deserves to be celebrated, even if you are not sure what to do with the feedback.

Make time to share about how the exercise felt and what happened for people as they engaged with the activities. Try asking questions like "What was that like for you?" or "What did you learn about yourself during that activity?" or simply "What would you like to share about what is happening for you right now?" Asking the group to share what they would like to can allow individuals to disclose what they feel comfortable sharing, while letting other group members choose not to share. If you notice that some group members are quick to share or talk over others, try setting ground rules for sharing, or try inviting group members to share by name, selecting those who appear to want to speak but who do not often get the chance to. If you have a time limit for sharing, try to let people know about that time limit so they can make choices about how much information they would like to disclose and the emotional depth they would like to access with others.

Try responding to others by saying "Thank you for sharing" or with compassionate witnessing. Compassionate witnessing is a way of responding based on what happened inside of you as the other person shared. For example, "When you shared, I felt sad and noticed a heaviness in my chest," or "I'm finding myself curious and interested. If we had time I would want to know more." Responding in these ways allows people to share their inner experiences without being treated like a problem to fix, and it helps to avoid advice-giving and problem-solving.

Notes

1. To learn more about the triangle of experience, check out Accelerated Experiential Dynamic Psychotherapy (AEDP).

2. Dennis Dailey, "Sexual Expression and Ageing," in *The Dynamics of Ageing: Original Essays on the Processes and Experiences of Growing Old*, ed. D. Berghorn and D. Schafer (Boulder, CO: Westview, 1981), 311–30.

3. Audre Lorde, *Sister Outsider* (Berkeley: Ten Speed, 2007), 55–57.

HILLARY L. McBRIDE (PhD, University of British Columbia) is a registered psychologist, an award-winning researcher, and a sought-after speaker who specializes in embodiment. She formerly cohosted *The Liturgists* podcast, hosts the *Other People's Problems* podcast, and has appeared on other popular podcasts. McBride's clinical and academic work has been recognized by the American Psychological Association and the Canadian Psychological Association. She teaches graduate students in counseling psychology and has a private practice in Victoria, British Columbia. Learn more at www.hillarylmcbride.com.